I Love ME!

Colorful and Creative

I Love Me! Colorful and Creative

Author Niyah La'Don and Takiyah
Designer Niyah La'Don and Takiyah

Copyright Single Mom And The City 2020

ISBN: 978 0 578 81169 7

Single Mom And The City supports copyright. Copyright fuels creativity and creates a vibrant culture. Thank you for buying an authorized edition of I Love Me! Colorful and Creative, and complying fully with copyright laws by not reproducing, scanning, or distributing any part of this book without permission. Thank you for the support of authors and designers.

Any reproduction of any content in this book is prohibited without the written consent of the authors. No part of this book may be reproduced.

Published in the United States of America

A happy girl filled with joy and wonder is always beautiful.

*Perfection is an illusion. Be the best version of yourself.
Beauty is being yourself.*

The best you can do is get good at being you.

*Remember, you are the descendant of royalty.
You are a Princess.*

Follow your hearts desire.

Well-read and well-versed. A winning combination.
Now that's Powerful.

Follow your dreams. The bigger, the better.

Be focused. Be determined. Be empowered.

*My melanin is magic. I can't quite explain it.
It's that extra special something that makes me amazing.*

Positive. Powerful. Phenomenal.

I am confident. 100% exquisite.

Self love is the best love.

A girl that is happy and confident is always beautiful.

Brainy. Beautiful. Brilliant.

Sweet, Spicy and Smart. Live life on your own terms.

Unapologetic. Unmatched. Unbelievable. Unique.

Excellence. Brilliance. Flawless. Shine bright light a diamond.

I expect the best. Nothing less. The End.

My DNA is legendary.
DNA: deoxyribonucleic acid - The carrier of genetic information.

When you dream big, miracles happen.

I am an original! My only competition is me. Confidence from within will propel me to win.

Be you. Beautiful YOU.
Paint an intricate picture of the life you want, then create it!

You blessed the world with your innocence and beauty.
Curious. Inventive. Brilliant. Multifaceted. Talent Inconceivable.
You are destined for greatness!

www.ingramcontent.com/pod-product-compliance
Lightning Source LLC
Chambersburg PA
CBHW081157290426
44108CB00018B/2580